Ode on Darwen

Nick Monks

Bluebell Publishing

For Amanda, Karl, Saskia

Title Page

Ode on Darwen- Nick Monks

Published August 2020

Printed by Lulu

www.lulu.com

ISBN: 978-1-8381263-1-5

CONTENTS

PREFACE

Thatcher, Major, Blair did little or nothing to tackle poverty. Thatcher and Major believed an onus was on the deprived and disadvantaged to find jobs and improve themselves in an in theory buoyant economy. Blair made great strides with child poverty and pensioners poverty. But shrugged his shoulders in perplexity at adult poverty.

Many people who live in here Darwen work hard have value based family life's.   The details in this poems though are real. Unlike some Geraldine Monk and American poets like Ted Berringer/ CJ Wright/Anne Carson (Canadian)

I don't render much the subjects consciousness. Except in a few of the poems. The rejection of the poor. Which has been dealt new blows with universal credit and increased self- awareness from the subject thanks to the internet and information. Played a major role in the Brexit movement amongst other factors. The poems should be enjoyed as testament to human resilience and spirit.

Ode on Darwen

Sunbathing

Terrible sun in July
Janice comes out to sunbath
On the patch of grass behind Bargain Booze
She spreads a towel
Adds sun block to her arms
And reads a book. The high July sun straying over her.

Saturday Night

Darwen comes tapping on the door at 8am
So much hope. So much promised. So anticipated
Alas there are just ruins
Take aways lining the street. For those with dosh
The neon cascading outwards to illuminate the troubled
Passers-by with their problems carried like heavy bags

Some go tut pub. The guys and gals, and shout and beam
smiles
Suppin on acrid tasting beer and sipping Bacardi and Coke
When yer stagger om. The toxic depressants deadening yer
brain. A hollow numbing out of

At five pm. The traffic is gridlocked on the devils A666
Schoolkids two of whom have already come out queer
Boisterously shriek around an anonymous unknown statue
on the grass

Janice, Carol and James av bin thinking- they gaze down the
A666
Nor nowts changed.

The Yellow Skip

The locals circulate
The damp weed filled alleyway
Between one row and the next

There as inviting as a room with wine, candles and snacks
Is a brightened yellow skip

They come in turns to rummage through the debris
Test the mattress for usability
The two tyres could be worth dosh says Janice to Dawn
Finally throwing stuff out ont cracked tarmac Keith finds a
Battery charger. Chuffed tut bits ee takes it om
A tatty small rucksack will do for Amelia says Chrissi

When the night comes the starlings peck at the stale bread
Mice and rats forage climbing up on a stray electrical lead

Then the next day when the man comes to hoist the skip
Away Chris and Matt are ready for im.

Touching Daffodils

Emma comes out. She's got Ralph and Davina
With her as support
Nervously watching for attackers
They plant daffodil bulbs in the soil next tut house

The daffodils are yellow like the sun or an unusual dawn sky
They bloom like flickering stars

While in the playing fields kids are throwing stones at a barn
owl
"To help it fly away"

And the "host of golden daffodils." bloom in spring
While Stochakovich new symphony of the barren and the
bleak
Is drowned out by Lionel Richie songs still playing at 4am

Disco at 4am

At 4am the music of Lionel Richie and Marvin Gaye
Then the drum solo of Santana
Completes the thesis on freedom of the will
Half an hour later it's time for sex
All heard through paper thin terraced house walls.

The Pawn Shop

The pawn shop on the A666
Is the only shop without a George cross flag
It represents a town treasure
The pawn shop is where people come to chat
To quell and perdite their problems
More connected and urban and in touch
Than the NHS monstrosity
The pawn shop caters to food and rent poverty
Strewn healing balms across the needy like card glitter.

Assessment Centre

Here Ian Duncan Smith (beware the quiet man)
Transforms people's life's
Ex mental health nurses assess
The tortured, the in trouble, the cant cope, the maladied,
And unless the actors are as good as Montgomery Clift
Finds them fit for work
And slashes their welfare payments.

Mental Health Day Centre (Business Training)

Here renamed from a drop into a
Business Training College
Emma, Rose and Hilda and Mark
Decided to make a calendar and put poems in it
Hilda's brother in law runs a printing press
Refugees from IT training. From secretarial courses
And the woodwork coarse- (Run by a depressed man)
Swelled the numbers of the card and calendar business to 34

In the IT training coarse the mental health nurses
Teach how to put numbers into boxes- spreadsheets
And print text on a printer
The hilarious joke is that nobody is doing a thing to lead to a job
But the statistics are good and vital to the government
Who tick the boxes- 89 people in quality work related training
And Emma, Hilda, Janice, Mark. Have fun, sneer, vent, cry
And drink coffee. Then one more cup. Perhaps a biscuit.
Before the calendar with a poem for each month
Is sent to the printers and on sale to the public
34 people thus in employment and training.

Christmas in Darwen

Snow petals falling over the maddened roofs
Of the street sleeping
Tomorrow they'll be motorbike revving
And trips tut shops to buy electricity ont card
Feuds over car parking
And the town centre will be a lit by Christmas tree lights.

Deprivation

Thousands of terrible crowds of soldiers
Coming back from Dunkirk
And the police are called out to a domestic at No 71
As the pound shops open
And thousands of people on sleeping pills
Realize their dream of a bacon and egg breakfast is-
No way. And the £1 clock from pound land
Dupes them into thinking its 7am when its 10 am
Oh to have an Ikea bookcase. A Rolex watch. Faberge
perfume. A Bosch electric shaver. A super duper
Sleepeezee king sized bed.

Moving House

If you arrived here from a farm
In the moors around Clitheroe
They would make you ill within 24 hours
But how would you live with not enough
Money for frozen chips. Or a cooker or a freezer
Grilling the chips on the new ZX40 Zanussi
Dual microwave grill. Bought from gumtree for £15
Carried back from Feniscowles in a taxi.

Thatcher, Major, Blair

First there was Thatcher
Then Major
Then Blair
At the end of a lifetime project
Inflicting on me by bureaucrats
Who think they have the right to harm me
And did
Well over half of British don't have any toe hold
At all. In the age of consumerism.

From There to Here in Darwen

In the industrial revolution
People wore clogs
And worked in cotton mills
Now they can't afford food
And sit in dingy one room bedrooms
Designed for cotton mill families
And fall on right wing Brexit nationalism.

Insomnia

At 10.12 pm the room clicks and turns black
There is no electricity
The 24 hour petrol station
Doesn't do electricity top ups
So you sleep. But can't and wait for morning light
And for the Co Op to open at 7 am
Were you go racked by insomnia and fatigued by no sleep.

Considering Emigration

Once there were fields
Over the plains of Darwen
Darwen moor stood colossal and regal
Let's emigrate to Ormskirk
Let's trail across the A666 along the traffic jams
To the food bank where we can get pasta.

Sunday Walk

On a Sunday Bert, Tracey and the five young uns
Go to walk to the top of Darwen moor
The lower fields path is muddy
Others in the freezing air are walking to the summit
Below like a grey river of doom
Lies Darwen like a river with no water. Just doom.

Darwen Credo

They scratched your new car
Owned for four days
Ridiculed and lambasted you
These are my love sonnets on Darwen
And the car is all in have to get to church
And writers events. And I have no money-
For food and am in debt. And can't make the bills
They scratched my new car. That my parents gave me
That I have only owned for four days
When I left it parked for 15 minutes
In the spirit filled ordained streets of regal Darwen
Below the wild beautiful Darwen Moor.

Darwen Sonnets

1

We live. Beer please
Wi get nowt us
Bloody jag
Smash is windows, I say
Av got to go tut work
Suncream ont deck chairs int yard
What time are yer at work
6am cleaning floors of Lidl
If wi get a car
Wi can sit int traffic jams on A666
Why they call it 666 after devil
Mi mums got bunions and cancer and dementia
Thousands of stars explode in cascading
Light overt Darwen moors.
UKIP tells the truth does that Nigel Farage
Ang em up. Wi get nowt us
Thousands of unnamed bleeding birds rendered
Over the moors of Darwen
Lets emigrate to Warrington
Nor pass mi another beer
Av wi to get out, lol
Do you think mi er is beautiful
I'll vote conservative. Billy brag says: oh I cant remember.

2

Trees were once here
Over the land of Bert and Bill
Trees logging
Were you off to. To cut down a friggin Christmas tree
I'm a lumber jack and I'm alright
But I can't afford another beer
I like Justine Timberlake mi
I like Rachael Welsh / not a boob job man me
Stars so bloody many of em
Am off to play three and in. Your bloody 37 pal
Lets sunbathe at night
Across the verdant fields of catholic schools
Thousands of dead red blood deadened birds
Over the foothills of Darwen moors
Lets emigrate to Lancaster
Slurp
Ees in for it im
Thousands of dead birds shot by slug gun pellets

3

Put washing ont line
Sing song, honey for dinner

Theresa May sits on the veranda of her three acre lawn

Listening to Verdi Aida
While bodkin Boris plays cricket cracking a joke about
transvestites to and Etonian friend

Use chip fat, if yuv run out of sun cream luv
A like em small. Pervert you are.

4

Honey am off to work
For British rail
Buy some toilet paper and a camera memory card ont way
back

There are eight pound shops in Darwen
We fall deeper down
Until only arguments can surface us into the heat
Of the hatred of Theresa Fays anointed eyes
Lullabies on Darwen moor

Save housing Is a red tent betwixt Darwen Tower and Great
Hill
In the bounteous mud

Ees funny that Andrew Carr, ont Countdown show
Right wing little Hitlers stoke the ravid death songs

She's middle class she is, a prostitute professional
Babies lined up. If they can't curtsy at the appropriate
moment
Ian Duncan Smith will spit on them
You need hand grenades to walk through Darwen centre
Edith sits knitting a teddy bear
Ee geezer did you try to talk to me
There's a sand pit in Darwen cemetery
You sod, I'd like to go to Benidorm
Snow- flakes on mirrors
E- mail MP's with roses and pound shop ice cream
Oos Francois Macron oos Jimmy Tarbuck
Oos muddy oos.
There is no poverty everybody dude, pal as water an
electricity
A simulacrum of roofing and free hay fromt hay bales int
fields of Darwen's mountains
UKIP are marching up sleepy high street are your coming
Or rain bathing again
Free baths, please bring ID
Ees only after you boob job
Honey should I dress in black for the rest of my short life
Oos died on the fields of the Somme
The white stallion charger of Norman Hammond
Viciousness precedes total resignation
Salvation Army oo they kidding. Alan Carr chatty man
Sleep int loft
Sunbath with tar if you can't afford chip fat
1909 poverty, 2018 even more poverty

Scratch is car. Be careful you don't damage the plate folk
while your....
You you you. Dressage for extremism
I'll marry you if you'd only bloody ask. And wear a woolly
jumper fromt Primark
"Out tut devil with sellotaped shoes"
Don't think they'll drug you up and section you again.

5

Sing sing a song. Sing it loud. Sing it strong
Why are there 10,000 English flags ont side of buildings
Go tut abattoir and steal a frozen chicken
Slippage of time on Beijing websites
American amazon- free holidays to the suburbs of Benidorm
You poncey centralist. Liberalism what
Serenading line dances at the sunbed Methodist church

The Perfume of Abattoirs

Fragrance of a life well lived
Wasp honey
No seat space at the 9.30 mass
Girl in front of me breast feeding
A sports car racing away to reach the end
Of the flat earth
Insomnia can be cured by washing your mouth out with soap
Rows of death houses
Communication breakdown, only non- communitive is
Psychiatrically considered normal
Building a tent for £50k, took 11 months
Laughter from room 107 on the top floor
Government officials are looking into
Banning late modernist poetry
If you can't afford chip fat use washing up liquid
To sunbathe on the lilo in the back yard
Instant connections on the web
Instantaneous disconnective-ness from 34pence in the bank
account
There so friendly at the food bank
At the DWP the three door bouncers chew on a lunchtime
pasty
All animals are vigorously vetted and security checked by the
institute for auditing
An 87 million pound war jet over Darwin moor
A man shaking his fist at snow.

Political Speaker

A man stands on a soap box
"Globalism must be resisted
And nation states must assert proud independence"
The crowd Bill, Keith, Bob- go to a grocery store
And they come back with tomatoes and
Rotting cabbage to throw at him
Five school children dance in a ring
Two girls have blue hair and have chosen lesbianism
An old lady pulling a shopping bag on wheels
Barges past the crowd
Five policemen and seven police vehicles watch
Off with you off with you off with you- shout the crowd
A dead seagull falls from the air
The Darweners conclude it can't be eaten.

Darwen, Shopping

In the market place
People trail looking to harm others
Making comments
Chewing gum
Avin arguments
Seven are ongoing at any one time
Resounding like Verdi's Aida
"Don't talk like that to me"
"Are you looking at me or chewing a brick"
In the supermarket
"Just stop winging and help"
"Your so disorganized" in a raised voice
Round the corner three male teenagers
Are busy letting down the tyres of a 2005 Jaguar
That Keith bought with his father's inheritance.

The Anthem of Darwen Blackburn

Oos Jeremy Corbyn
Oos Jeremy Corbyn
Oos Jeremy Corbyn
Shout ogy ogy ogy, oy oy oy
Ogy, oy
Ogy, oy
Ogy ogy ogy, oy oy oy.

Bastions of Civilization, Spec Savers

At least their dressed smartly
And talk nicely
And there's air conditioning
Some of em come in to av a holiday
And the carpets are clean
Vicky and Dawn and Tracey
All live with their parents and work here
Only GPs and the CAB know the reality
Of squalor in Darwen, Blackburn.

Ode on Darwen 1

You arrived parked the car
In the only space you could find- luckily there was a space
A man was in a sleeping bag in a doorway
A red sleeping bag- like lipstick or blood or a red cardigan
Away out raised voices shouted
Cascading like drug use or police sirens or a Himalayan
waterfall
Even the feral pigeons don't come here
Not since and since and since- the man in tweed
And the lady with £1000 trousers implemented their policies
In their *Social Justice-Transforming Peoples Life's* document
We buy lager with chasers and sing rugby songs
At 4am it is time for the night watch furtive rats
While a beautiful badger scampers at the foot of Darwin
Moor
And the terrible sleep snoring. She wakes in a start
And says "Lets av another baby"
The yellow skip- is trawled over by the locals
While int allotment some find peace
One day a Peregrine flew across Darwen moor- no one
noticed.

Sail Away

Kiss me quick- a blue liqueur with icing sugar
Send me away in a boat
Over the Rubicon- into the food banks
The making do/ the mending things
Out into the blue Atlantic, away to new lands.

Hope

The political progressives mention us in there chattering
As a footnote
Before they continue chattering

And when everything is cancelled
Only the lies of political corruption in 2018 will remain

And the hope of the inner cities
Stronger rising stronger ever higher than scrapers or
Tenement flats. We the poor embody hope.

Thrift

Cancel the subscription to Netflix
Cancel the amazon prime- the one amazon
Dupes people into- then takes their money
Cancel internet security
Cancel the one milk bottle daily

Cancel food
Accommodation
Clothes
Haircuts.

Morning

In the morning
After finally getting to sleep at 5am
Kids are climbing on the garage roofs
There is loud hollering
Across yard walls
And in the background
A motorbike revs repeatedly

Two police cars are parked outside a house
And sheets are hanging on yard washing lines
Most of the residents of Corporation Road
don't have cars
As Jeff opens the front door and walks to the shop
Malicious eyes glare from chinks in curtains.

Newsagent

You are thirsty. Have not drunk for five hours
You go in a newsagent
Ask for a glass of water
The guy looks at you with hatred
And says "Taps broke pal. "

Pubs

It's a Saturday night
Customers pile int pubs
The juke box drowns talk
And coarse laughter and groping
Are mixed with beer and spirits and dry white wine
At the end of the evening, drunks amble
Drunkenly plodding home. They think this is good.

Corner Shop

Darwen lies stretched
Along a valley
The A666
Gridlocked 24/7 352 days a year.

You chose Darwen Asylum
Thinking you could set up a corner shop
You and Serena and the three kids.

Ode on Darwen 2

Eer Daphne. What's for tea
Leave mi alone am doin mI nails
Keith clambers the stairs
Launches himself on the bed
And watches the mounted wall television
Daphne curls her hair
They tin open a Heinz tin of minestrone soup
It plops like chemical slime into the unclean pan
And put on the radio
Playing *West End Boys* by The Pet Shop Boys
Keith goes out after tea to play snooker
As he leaves the hall he shouts
Your not pregnant are you again
Daphne doesn't answer she cries
As thousands of ants scurry in the kitchen floor

A ray of light appears through the broken blinds
Of the lounge in the two up two down
On Corporation Road. She turns up the volume
Of the radio to drown out motorbike revving
Rain falls lightly on the yard washing line cloths.

Long Ago in Darwen

As Elizabeth is putting the dress and the breaches
Through the mangle
Chalking the two door- steps at 8pm
One of these new posh cars can be heard
Along Darwen High Street
The five children under martial control
Are asleep or should be
And unnoticed unseen black green and white angels
Are soaring and cavorting on lace wings over Darwen High
Moor

Bin Day

Its bin day!
Time of avarice and meanness
Only paralleled by car parking issues
Karl knocks over your bin
Placed outside the back gate
Then rethinks and jams it against the gate latch
So you can't get out

The bin men are executive high- flyers
Compared to the mealy residents on Corporation Road
And Karl, Christine and Chris stand with blank eyes
Of malice looking at the highly intelligent bin men
Taking away the rubbish of Corporation Road, Darwen
But sadly leaving the residents stranded behind.

Ode on Darwen 3

Eer Kevin. The cooker won't work
Wiv no chip fat. The gas meters cut out
Buy some cheese and pickle baguettes from Subway
When you go to get gas credits
How many cigarettes are left? Four!. Ring Jeffrey-
Ask for a loan. And let's watch tv tonight
We can't afford the pub. Are ye avin a laugh
There's thousands wi no money.

An English cross of saint George hangs from the pole
Screwed to the side of the house
Keith shaves with his wife's razor. Slaps on vim aftershave
He dances to the radio playing "Lucky Man" by Verve
And walks in track suit bottoms to the bookies
Were the Brexiteers chatter. In the diming Darwen evening.

www.ingramcontent.com/pod-product-compliance
Lightning Source LLC
Chambersburg PA
CBHW070033110426
42741CB00035B/2750